The Secret of Believing Prayer

The Secret of Believing Prayer

Andrew Murray

BETHANY HOUSE PUBLISHERS
MINNEAPOLIS, MINNESOTA 55438
A Division of Bethany Fellowship, Inc.

Originally published under the titles *Have Faith in God* and *In My Name*

The Secret of Believing Prayer
Andrew Murray

Library of Congress Catalog Card Number 80-69320

ISBN 0-87123-590-0

Published by Bethany Fellowship, Inc.
6820 Auto Club Road, Minneapolis, Minnesota 55438

Printed in the United States of America

ANDREW MURRAY was born in South Africa in 1828. After receiving his education in Scotland and Holland, he returned to that land and spent many years there as both pastor and missionary. He was a staunch advocate of biblical Christianity. He is best known for his many devotional books.

Contents

CHAPTER ONE

The Secret of Believing Prayer

> Jesus, answering, said unto them, *Have faith in God.* Verily I say unto you, Whosoever shall not doubt in his heart, but shall believe that what he saith cometh to pass; he shall have it. Therefore I say unto you, All things whatsoever ye pray and ask for, believe that ye have received them, and ye shall have them.—Mark 11:22-24

The promise of answer to prayer is one of the most wonderful in all Scripture. In many hearts it has raised the question, "How can I ever attain the faith that knows that it receives all it asks?"

It is this question our Lord would answer today. When He gave that wonderful promise to His disciples, He spoke another word in which He points out where the faith in the answer to prayer rises from, and ever finds its strength. HAVE FAITH IN GOD: this word precedes the other, "Have faith in the promise of an answer to prayer."

The power to believe *a promise* depends entirely on faith in *the promiser.* Trust in the person begets trust in his word. It is only where we live and associate with God in a personal, loving relationship, where God himself is all to us, where our whole being is continually opened up and exposed to the mighty influences at work where His holy presence is revealed, that the capacity will be developed for believing that He gives whatever we ask.

This connection between faith in God and faith in His promise will become clear if we think what faith really is. It is often compared to the hand or the mouth by which we take and appropriate what is offered to us. But we should understand that faith is also the ear by which I hear what is promised, the eye by which I see what is offered me. The power to take depends on this. I must *hear* the person who gives me the promise—the very tone of his voice gives me courage to believe. I must *see* him—in the light of his eye and countenance, all fear passes away. The value of the promise depends on the promiser; it is on my knowledge of what the promiser is that faith in the promise depends.

For this reason, Jesus, when He gives that

wonderful prayer-promise, first says, "Have faith in God." That is, let your eye be open to the living God, and gaze on Him, seeing Him who is invisible. Through the eye I yield myself to the influence of what is before me; I allow it to enter, to exert its influence, to leave its impression upon my mind. So believing God is just looking to God and what He is, allowing Him to reveal His presence, yielding my time and my whole being to take in the full impression of what He is as God; it is my soul opened up to receive and rejoice in the overshadowing of His love.

Yes, faith is the eye to which God shows what He is and does. Through faith, the light of His presence and the workings of His mighty power stream into the soul. As that which I see lives in me, so by faith God lives in me too.

Faith is also the ear through which the voice of God is always heard and communication with Him maintained. Through the Holy Spirit the Father speaks to us; the Son is the Word, the substance of what God says; the Spirit is the living voice. The child of God needs the secret voice from heaven to teach him, as it taught Jesus, what to say and what to do. An ear opened toward God—a believing heart waiting to hear what He says—will hear Him speak.

The words of God will not only be the words of a Book, but, proceeding from the mouth of

God, they will be spirit and truth, life and power. They will produce in deed and experience what are otherwise only thoughts. Through this opened ear the soul tarries under the influence of the life and power of God himself. As the words I hear enter my mind and dwell and work there, so through faith God enters my heart and dwells and works there.

When faith is in full exercise as eye and ear, as the faculty of the soul by which we see and hear God, then it will be able to exercise its full power as hand and mouth to appropriate God and His blessings. The power of reception will depend entirely on the power of spiritual perception. For this reason Jesus said, "Have faith in God."

Faith is simply surrender: yielding myself to the impression the words I hear make on me. By faith *I yield myself to the living God*. His glory and love fill my heart and have the mastery over my life. Faith is fellowship: giving myself up to the influence of the friend who makes me a promise, and becoming linked to him. When we enter into this living fellowship *with God himself*, in faith that sees and hears Him, it becomes easy and natural to believe His promise regarding prayer. Faith in the promise is the fruit of faith in the promiser; the prayer of faith is rooted in the life of faith.

In this way, the faith that prays effectually is

indeed a gift of God. Not as something that He bestows or infuses but as the blessed disposition or habit of soul which is wrought and grows up in a life of communion with Him. Surely for one who knows his Father well, and lives in constant close fellowship with Him, it is a simple thing to believe the promise that He will do the will of His child who lives in union with himself.

Because many of God's children do not understand this connection between the life of faith and the prayer of faith, their experience of the power of prayer is very limited. When they desire earnestly to obtain an answer from God, they fix their whole heart upon the promise, and try their utmost to grasp that promise in faith. When they do not succeed, they are ready to give up hope; the promise is true, but it is beyond their power to take hold of it in faith. Listen to the lesson Jesus teaches us: "Have faith in God," the living God. Let faith look to God more than the thing promised; His love, His power, His living presence will awaken and work the faith.

To one asking for some means to gain strength in his arms and hands, a physician would say that his whole body must be built up and strengthened. So the cure of feeble faith is found in the invigoration of one's whole spiritual life by communing with God. Learn to believe God, to take hold of God, to let God take possession of your life; then it will be easy to take hold of the promise. He that knows and trusts God finds it easy to trust the promise too.

Note how evident this was in the saints of old. Every special exhibition of the power of faith was the fruit of a special revelation of God. See it in Abraham: "And the word of the Lord came unto Abram, saying, Fear not, Abram; I am thy shield. And He brought him forth abroad, and said. . . . *And he believed* the Lord."

In a later instance, "the Lord appeared unto him and said unto him, I am God Almighty. And Abram fell on his face, and God talked with him, saying, As for me, behold my covenant is with thee." It was the revelation of God himself that gave the promise living power to enter Abraham's heart and build faith.

Because he knew God, Abraham could do nothing but trust His promise. God's promise will be to us what God himself is. It is the man who walks before the Lord, and falls upon his face to listen while God speaks to him, who will receive the promise. Though we have God's promises in the Bible, with full liberty to take them, spiritual power is wanting unless God himself speaks them to us. And He speaks to those who walk and live with Him.

Therefore, *have faith in God*; let faith be all eye and ear. Surrender to let God make His full impression, and reveal himself fully in your soul. Count it one of the chief blessings of prayer to exercise faith in God, as the living mighty God who waits to fulfill in us all the good pleasure of His will, with power. See Him as the God of Love, who delights to bless us and impart himself. In such worship of God, power will speedily come to believe the promise, "All things whatsoever ye ask, believe that ye receive." In faith make God your own; the promise will be yours as well.

We seek God's gifts; God wants to give us *himself* first. We think of prayer as the power to draw down good gifts from heaven, and Jesus as the means to draw ourselves up to God. We want to stand at the door and cry; Jesus would have us enter in and realize that we are friends and children.

Let every experience of the littleness of your faith in prayer urge you first to have and exercise more faith in the living God, and in such faith to yield yourself to Him. A heart full of God has power for the prayer of faith. Faith in God begets faith in the promise—the promise of an answer to prayer.

Therefore, child of God, take time to bow before Him, to wait on Him to reveal himself. Take time and let your soul, in holy awe and worship, exercise and express its faith in the Infinite One. As He imparts himself and takes possession of you, the prayer of faith will crown your faith in God.

"Lord, teach us to pray."

O my God, I do believe in Thee. I believe in Thee as the Father, infinite in Thy love and power. And as the Son, my Redeemer and my Life. And as the Holy Spirit, Comforter and Guide and Strength. Three-One God, I have faith in Thee. I know and am sure that all that Thou art Thou art to me, that all Thou hast promised Thou wilt perform.

Lord Jesus, increase this faith. Teach me to take time to wait and worship in your holy presence until my faith takes in all there is in my God for me. Let it see Him as the fountain of all life, working with almighty strength to accomplish His will on the world and in me. Let it see Him in His love longing to meet and fulfill my desires. Let it so take possession of my heart and life that through faith God alone may dwell there. Lord Jesus, help me! With my whole heart would I believe in God. Let faith in God each moment fill me.

My Blessed Saviour, how can Thy Church glorify Thee? How can it fulfill that work of intercession through which Thy kingdom must come unless our whole life be faith in God? Blessed Lord, speak Thy Word, "Have faith in God," into the depths of my soul. Amen.

CHAPTER TWO

The Cure of Unbelief

> Then came the disciples to Jesus apart,
> and said, Why could not we cast him out? And
> Jesus said unto them, *Because of your un-*
> *belief*: for verily I say unto you, *If ye have faith*
> as a grain of mustard seed, *nothing shall be*
> *impossible* to you. Howbeit this kind goeth not
> out but *by prayer and fasting.*—Matt.
> 17:19-21

When the disciples saw Jesus cast the evil
spirit out of the epileptic whom "they could not
cure," they asked the Master for the cause of
their failure. He had given them power and
authority over all devils and all diseases. They
had often exercised that power, and joyfully told
how the devils were subject to them. Yet now,
while He was on the Mount, they had utterly
failed.

There had been nothing in the will of God or in the nature of the case to render deliverance impossible—at Christ's bidding the evil spirit had gone out. From their expression "Why could we not?", it is evident that they had wished and sought to do so; they had probably used the Master's name and commanded the evil spirit to go out. Their efforts had been vain, and, in front of the multitude, they had been put to shame.

Christ's answer was direct and plain: "Because of your unbelief." His success and their failure was not due to some special power unavailable to them. He had so often taught them that there is one power, that of faith, to which everything, in the kingdom of darkness, as in the kingdom of God, must bow; in the spiritual world, failure has but one cause: lack of faith.

Faith is the one condition on which all divine power can enter into man and work through him. It is the susceptibility of the unseen—man's will yielded to, and molded by, the will of God. The power the disciples had received to cast out devils, they did not hold in themselves as a permanent gift or possession; the power was in Christ, to be received, and held, and used by faith alone. Had they been full of faith *in Him* as Lord and Conqueror of the spirit-world, had they been full of faith *in Him* as having given them authority to cast out in His Name, they would have had victory. "Because of your unbelief" was, for all time, the Master's explanation and reproof of impotence and failure in His Church.

Such lack of faith must have a cause. The disciples might have asked, "And why could we not believe? Our faith has cast out devils before this. Why have we now failed in believing?"

The Master proceeds to tell them, "This kind goeth not out but by fasting and prayer." As faith is the simplest, so it is the highest exercise of the spiritual life, where one's spirit yields itself in perfect receptivity to God's Spirit, and is thus strengthened to its highest activity. This faith depends entirely upon the state of the spiritual life; only when this is strong and in full health, when the Spirit of God has full sway in one's life, is there the power of faith to do mighty deeds. Therefore Jesus adds, "Howbeit this kind goeth not out but by fasting and prayer."

The faith that can overcome such stubborn resistance as you have just seen in this evil spirit, Jesus tells them, is not possible except to men living in very close fellowship with God and in very special separation from the world—in prayer and fasting. Therefore He teaches us two lessons in regard to prayer. One, that faith needs a life of prayer in which to grow and keep strong. The other, that prayer needs fasting for its full and perfect development.

Faith needs a life of prayer for its full growth. In all the different aspects of the spiritual life, there is such union, such unceasing action and reaction, that each may be both cause and effect. Thus it is with faith. There can be no true prayer without faith; some measure of faith must precede prayer. Yet, prayer is also the way to more faith; there can be no higher degrees of faith except through more prayer.

Nothing needs to grow so much as our faith. "Your faith groweth exceedingly" is said of one church. When Jesus spoke the words "According to your faith be it unto you," He announced the law of the kingdom, which tells us that not all have equal degrees of faith, that the same person does not always have the same degree, and that the measure of faith always determines the measure of power and of blessing.

If we want to know where and how our faith is to grow, the Master points us to the throne of God. It is in prayer, the exercise of faith in fellowship with the living God, that faith can increase. Faith can live only by feeding on what is divine, on God himself.

It is in the adoring worship of God, the deep silence of soul that yields itself for God to reveal himself, that the capacity for knowing and trusting God will be developed. It is as we take His word from the Blessed Book, and bring it to Him, asking Him to speak it to us with His living, loving voice, that the power will come fully to believe and receive the word as God's own word to us. It is in prayer, in living contact with God, that faith—the power to trust God and to accept everything He says, to accept every possibility He has offered to our faith—will become strong in us.

Many Christians cannot understand what is meant by the "much prayer" they sometimes hear spoken of; they can form no conception, nor do they feel the need, of spending hours with God. But what the Master says, the experience of His people has confirmed: men of strong faith are men of much prayer.

This just brings us back again to the lesson we learned when Jesus first said, "Have faith in God." It is God, the living God, into whom our faith must strike its roots deep and broad; then it will be strong enough to remove mountains and cast out devils. "If ye have faith, nothing shall be impossible to you."

If we would give ourselves up to the work God has for us in the world, coming into contact with the mountains and the devils that must be cast away and cast out, we would soon comprehend the need for much faith and for much prayer— the soil in which faith can be cultivated. Christ Jesus is our life, the life of our faith too. It is His life in us that makes us strong, and makes us simple to believe.

The spirit of faith will come in power through dying to self—a necessity for much prayer and closer union with Jesus. *Faith needs prayer* for its full growth.

Prayer also needs fasting for its full growth. Prayer is the one hand with which we grasp the invisible; fasting, the other, with which we let loose and cast away the visible. In nothing is man more closely connected with the world of sense than in his need of food and his enjoyment of it. It was the fruit, good for food, with which man was tempted in Paradise. It was with bread to be made of stones that Jesus, when hungry, was tempted in the wilderness; in fasting He triumphed.

The body has been redeemed to be a temple of the Holy Spirit; in body as well as spirit, but especially, Scripture says, in eating and drinking, we are to glorify God. There are many Christians to whom eating to the glory of God has not yet become a spiritual reality.

The first thought suggested by Jesus' words in regard to fasting and prayer is that only in a life of moderation, temperance, and self-denial will there be the heart or the strength to pray much.

There is also its more literal meaning. Sorrow and anxiety cannot eat; joy celebrates its feasts with eating and drinking. There may come times of intense desire when it seems obvious that the body, with its appetites, lawful though they be, still hinder the spirit in its battle with the powers of darkness; the need is felt of keeping the body under.

We are creatures of the senses; our mind is helped by what comes to us embodied in concrete form; fasting helps to express, to deepen, and to confirm the resolution that we are ready to sacrifice anything—even ourselves—to attain what we seek for the kingdom of God. He who accepted the fasting and sacrifice of the Son values, accepts, and rewards with spiritual power the soul that is thus ready to give up all for Christ and His kingdom.

There follows a still wider application. Prayer is the reaching out after God and the unseen; fasting, the letting go of all that is seen and temporal. Ordinary Christians imagine that all that is not positively forbidden and sinful is lawful to them, and seek to retain as much as possible of this world, with its property, literature, and enjoyments. But the truly consecrated soul is a soldier who carries only what he needs for warfare. Laying aside every weight, as well as the easily besetting sin, afraid of entangling himself with the affairs of this life, he seeks to lead a Nazarite life, as one specially set apart for the Lord and His service. Without such voluntary separation, even from what is lawful, no one will attain power in prayer. "This kind goeth not out but by fasting and prayer."

Disciples of Jesus, who have asked the Mas-

ter to teach you to pray, come now and accept
His lessons. He tells you that prayer is the path
to faith, strong faith, that can cast out devils. He
tells you, "If ye have faith, nothing shall be impossible to you." Let this glorious promise en-
courage you to pray much.

Is the prize not worth the price? Shall we not
give up all to follow Jesus in the path He opens
to us? Shall we not, if necessary, fast? Shall we
not do anything that prevents the body or the
world around from hindering us in our great life-
work—having communion with God in prayer
that we may become men of faith whom He can
use in His work of saving the world?

"LORD, TEACH US TO PRAY."

*Lord Jesus, how continually Thou hast to re-
prove me for my unbelief! How strange it must
appear to Thee, this terrible incapacity of trusting my Father and His promises. Lord, let Thy
reproof, with its searching "Because of your
unbelief," sink into the very depths of my heart
and reveal to me how much of the sin and suffering around me is my blame. And then teach me,
Blessed Lord, that there is a place where faith
can be learned and gained—even in prayer and
fasting that brings me into living and abiding
fellowship with thyself and the Father.*

O Saviour, Thou thyself art the author and

the perfecter of my faith; teach me what it is to let Thee live in me by Thy Holy Spirit. Lord, my efforts and prayers for grace to believe have been so unavailing. I know why it was; I sought for strength in myself to be given from Thee. Holy Jesus, do at length teach me the mystery of Thy life in me, and how Thou, by Thy Spirit, dost undertake to live in me the life of faith, to see to it that my faith shall not fail. Let me see that my faith will just be a part of that wonderful prayer-life which Thou givest to them who expect their training for the ministry of intercession, not in word and thought only, but in the holy unction Thou givest by the inflowing of the Spirit of thine own life. And teach me how, in fasting and prayer, I may grow up to the faith to which nothing shall be impossible. Amen.

CHAPTER THREE

Prayer and Love

And whensoever ye stand praying, forgive, if ye have aught against any one; that your Father also which is in heaven may forgive you your trespasses.—Mark 11:25

These words immediately follow the great prayer-promise, "All things whatsoever ye pray, believe that ye have received them, and ye shall have them." We have already seen how the words that preceded that promise "have faith in God" show that, in prayer, all depends upon our relation to God being clear. These words that follow it remind us that our relation with fellow-men must be clear too. Love to God and love to our neighbor are inseparable; the prayer from a heart that is either not right with God or with men cannot prevail. Faith and love are interdependent.

This is a matter which our Lord frequently emphasized. In the Sermon on the Mount (Matt. 5:23, 24), when speaking of the sixth commandment, He taught His disciples that acceptable worship to the Father was impossible if everything were not right with the brother: "If thou art offering thy gift at the altar, and there rememberest that thy brother hath aught against thee, leave there thy gift before the altar, and go thy way; first be reconciled to thy brother, and then come and offer thy gift."

When speaking of prayer to God, after having taught us to pray, "Forgive us our debts, as we also have forgiven our debtors," Jesus added at the close of the prayer, "If you forgive not men their trespasses, neither will your Father forgive your trespasses."

At the close of the parable of the unmerciful servant Jesus applies His teaching in the words, "So shall also my heavenly Father do unto you, if ye forgive not every one his brother from your hearts."

Standing beside the dried-up fig tree, where He speaks of the wonderful power of faith and the prayer of faith, He all at once, apparently without connection, introduces the thought, "Whensoever ye stand praying, forgive, if ye have aught against any one; that your Father also which is in heaven may forgive you your trespasses." It seems the Lord had learned during His life at Nazareth and afterwards that disobedience to the law of love to men was the great sin even of praying people and the great cause of the feebleness of their prayer. It seems as if He wanted to lead us into His own blessed experience, for nothing gives such liberty of access, and such power in believing, as the consciousness that we have given ourselves in love and compassion for those whom God loves.

The first lesson taught here is the need for a forgiving disposition. We pray, "Forgive, *even as* we have forgiven." Scripture says, "Forgive one another, even as God also in Christ forgave you." God's full and free forgiveness is to be the standard for our forgiveness. Otherwise, our reluctant, half-hearted forgiveness, which is not forgiveness at all, will be God's rule with us.

Every prayer depends upon our faith in God's pardoning grace. If God dealt with us according to our sins, not one prayer could be heard. Pardon opens the door to all God's love and blessing; because God has pardoned all our sin, our prayer can prevail to obtain all we need. The deep sure ground of answer to prayer is God's forgiving love. When it has taken possession of the heart, we pray in faith. But also, when it has taken possession of the heart, we live in love. God's forgiving disposition, revealed in His love to us, becomes our disposition; as the power of His forgiving love is shed abroad and dwells within us, we forgive even as He forgives.

If great and grievous injury or injustice is done us, we seek first of all to possess a godlike disposition—to be kept from a sense of wounded honor, from a desire to maintain our rights, or from rewarding the offender as he has deserved. In the little annoyances of daily life, we are watchful not to excuse hasty temper, sharp words, or rash judgment, with the thought that we mean no harm, that we do not keep the anger long, or that it would be too much to expect from feeble human nature. Instead, we must forgive the way God and Christ do. We take the command literally, "*Even as* Christ forgave, *so also* do ye."

The blood that cleanses the conscience from dead works cleanses from selfishness too; the love it reveals is pardoning love, which takes possession of us and flows through us to others. Our forgiving love to men is the evidence of God's forgiving love in us, and therefore the condition of the prayer of faith.

There is a second, more general lesson: our daily life in the world comprises the rest of our communion with God in prayer. Often a Christian, when he comes to pray, does his utmost to cultivate a certain frame of mind which he thinks will please God. He misunderstands, or forgets, that life does not consist of so many loose pieces, of which now the one, then the other, can be taken up.

Life is a whole, and God judges the pious frame of the hour of prayer according to the ordinary frame of the daily life—of which the hour of prayer is but a small part. The tone of my life during the day, not the feeling I call up, is God's criterion of what I really am and desire. My drawing nigh to God is integral with my relationship to men and earth; failure here will cause failure there. This occurs not only when there is the distinct consciousness of something wrong between my neighbor and me; the ordinary current of my thinking and judging, the unloving thoughts and words I allow to pass unnoticed, can hinder my prayer.

The effectual prayer of faith comes out from a life given up to the will and the love of God. My prayer is dealt with by God, not according to what I try to be when I am praying, but when I am not praying.

There is also a third lesson: in our life with men, the one thing on which everything depends is *love*. The spirit of forgiveness is the spirit of love. Because God is love, He forgives; it is only when we are dwelling in love that we can forgive as God forgives.

Love to the brethren is the evidence of love to the Father, the ground of confidence before God, and the assurance that our prayer will be heard (1 John 4:20, 3:18-21, 23). "Let us love in deed and truth; *hereby* shall we assure our heart before him. If our heart condemn us not, we have boldness toward God, and whatever we ask, we receive of him." Neither faith nor work will profit if we have no love; it is love that unites with God, it is love that proves the reality of faith. As essential as the condition that precedes the great prayer-promise in Mark 11:24, "Have faith in God," is this one that follows it, "Have love to men." Right relations to the living God above me and the living men around me are the conditions of effectual prayer.

This love is of special consequence when we labor and pray for them. We sometimes give ourselves to work for Christ from zeal for His cause, or for our own spiritual health, without giving ourselves in personal self-sacrificing love for those whose souls we seek. No wonder that our faith is feeble and does not conquer. We must look on each wretched one, however unlovable he be, in the light of the tender love of Jesus the Shepherd seeking the lost; to see Jesus Christ in him, and to take him up, for Jesus' sake, in a heart that really loves—this is the secret of believing prayer and successful effort.

Jesus, in speaking of forgiveness, specifies love as its root. In the Sermon on the Mount He coupled His teaching and promises about prayer with the call to be merciful as the Father in heaven is merciful (Matt. 5:7, 8, 22, 38-48). We also see it here: a loving life is the condition of believing prayer.

It has been said, "There is nothing so heart-searching as believing prayer, or even the honest effort to pray in faith." Do not avoid the edge of that self-examination by the thought that God does not hear prayer for reasons known only to himself. By no means. "Ye ask and receive not, because ye ask amiss." Let that word of God search us. Let us ask whether our prayer is indeed the expression of a life wholly given over to the will of God and the love of man.

Love is the only soil in which faith can strike its roots and thrive. As it throws its arms up, and opens its heart heavenward, the Father always looks to see if it has them opened toward the evil and the unworthy too. In that love, not the love of perfect attainment but the love of fixed purpose and sincere obedience, faith can obtain the blessing.

He who gives himself to let the love of God dwell in him, and in the practice of daily life purposes to love as God loves, will have the power to believe in the Love that hears his every prayer. It is *the Lamb* who is in the midst of the throne; it is suffering and forbearing love that prevails with God in prayer. The merciful shall obtain mercy; the meek shall inherit the earth.

"Lord, Teach Us to Pray."

Blessed Father, Thou art Love, and only he that abideth in love abideth in Thee and in fellowship with Thee. The Blessed Son hath this day again taught me how deeply true this is of my fellowship with Thee in prayer. O my God, let Thy love, shed abroad in my heart by the Holy Spirit, be in me a fountain of love to all around me that out of a life in love may spring the power of believing prayer. My Father, grant by the Holy Spirit that this may be my experience, that a life in love to all around me be the gate to a life in the love of my God. Help me to find in the joy with which I forgive day by day whoever might offend me, the proof that Thy forgiveness to me is power and life.

Lord Jesus, my blessed teacher, teach me to forgive and to love. Let the power of Thy blood make the pardon of my sins such a reality that forgiveness, as shown by Thee to me, and by me to others, may be the very joy of heaven. Show me whatever in my relationships with fellowmen might hinder my fellowship with God, so that my daily life in my own home and in society may be the school in which strength and confidence are gathered for the prayer of faith. Amen.

CHAPTER FOUR

The Power of United Prayer

> Again I say unto you, That if two of you
> shall agree on earth as touching anything that
> they shall ask, *it shall be done* for them of my
> Father which is in heaven. For where two or
> three are gathered together in my name, there
> am I in the midst of them.—Matt. 18:19, 20

One of the first lessons our Lord taught in His
school of prayer was *not to be seen of men.* Enter
thy inner chamber; be alone with the Father.
When He has taught us that the meaning of
prayer is personal individual contact with God,
He comes with a second lesson: You have need
not only of secret prayer but also of public
united prayer.

He gives us a very special promise for the
united prayer of two or three who agree in what
they ask. As a tree's root is hidden in the ground

and its stem grows up into the sunlight, so prayer needs, for its full development, the secrecy in which the soul meets God alone, and the public fellowship with those who, in the name of Jesus, find their common meeting place.

The bond that unites a man to his fellowmen is no less real and close than that which unites him to God—he is one with them. Grace renews not only our relation to God but to man too. We learn to say not only "*My* Father" but "*Our* Father." Nothing would be more unnatural than for the children of a family to always meet their father separately, never in the united expression of their desires or their love.

Believers are members not only of one family but of one body. Each member of the body depends on the other, and the full action of the spirit dwelling in the body depends on the union and cooperation of all. So also, Christians cannot reach the full blessing God is ready to bestow through His Spirit unless they seek and receive it in fellowship with each other. In the union and fellowship of believers, the Spirit can manifest its full power. It was to the hundred and twenty continuing in one place together, and praying with one accord, that the Spirit came from the throne of the glorified Lord.

The marks of true united prayer are given us in these words of our Lord. The first is *agreement* as to the thing asked. There must not only be general consent on anything another may ask, there must also be a distinct united desire. The agreement must be, as all prayer, in spirit and in truth. In such agreement, it will become very clear to us what exactly we are asking, so that we may confidently ask according to God's will and may believe that we have received what we ask.

The second mark of united prayer is the gathering in, or into, the Name of Jesus. Here our Lord teaches that the Name must be the center of union to which believers gather, the bond of union that makes them one, just as a home contains and unites all who are in it. "The name of the Lord is a strong tower; the righteous runneth into it and is safe."

That Name is such a reality to those who understand and believe it that to meet within it is to have Jesus present. The love and unity of His disciples have infinite attraction to Jesus: "Where two or three are gathered in my name, *there am I in the midst of them.*" The living presence of Jesus, in the fellowship of His loving, praying disciples, gives united prayer its power.

The third mark of united prayer is the sure answer: "It shall be done for them of my Father." A prayer meeting for maintaining religious fellowship, or seeking personal edification, may have its use, but this was not the Saviour's purpose in instituting it. He meant it as a means of securing *special answers to prayer.*

A prayer meeting without recognized answers to prayer ought to be an anomaly. When any one of us has distinct desires for which we feel too weak to exercise the needful faith, we ought to seek strength in the help of others. In the unity of faith, love, and the Spirit, the power of the Name and the presence of Jesus acts more freely and the answer comes more surely. The evidence of true united prayer is the fruit, the answer, the receiving of the thing we have asked: "I say unto you, *It shall be done* for them of my Father which is in heaven."

What a privilege united prayer is, and what a power it could be. If the believing husband and wife knew that they were joined together in the Name of Jesus to experience His presence and power in united prayer (1 Peter); if friends believed what mighty help two or three praying in concert could give each other; if in every prayer meeting the coming together in the Name, the faith in the presence, and the expectation of the answer, were foremost; if in every church united effectual prayer were regarded as one of the chief purposes for which Christians are banded together—the highest exercise of their power as a church; if in the church universal the coming of the kingdom, and the King himself, first in the mighty outpouring of His Holy Spirit, then in His own glorious person, were matters of ceaseless united crying to God; who can say what blessing might come to, and through, those who thus agreed to prove God in the fulfillment of His promise?

The Apostle Paul is a very distinct example of faith in the power of united prayer. To the Romans he writes (15:30), "I beseech you, brethren, by the love of the Spirit, that ye *strive together with me* in your prayer to God for me." He expected to be delivered from his enemies and to prosper in his work.

He declared to the Corinthians (2 Cor. 1:11), "God will still deliver us, ye also helping together on our behalf by your supplications"; their prayer was to have a significant share in his deliverance. Of the Ephesians he requested, "With all prayer and supplication praying at all seasons in the Spirit for all the saints and on my behalf, that utterance may be given unto me." Power and success in his ministry depended on their prayers.

Paul informed the Philippians (1:19) that he expected his trials would turn to his salvation and the progress of the gospel "through your supplications and the supply of the Spirit of Jesus Christ." He challenged the Colossians (4:3) to continue steadfast in prayer, "Withal praying for us too, that God may open unto us a door for the word."

Paul urged the Thessalonians (2 Thess. 3:1), "Finally, brethren, pray for us, that the word of the Lord may run and be glorified, and that we may be delivered from unreasonable men." It is evident that Paul considered himself the member of a body, on the sympathy and cooperation of which he was dependent; he counted on the prayers of the churches to gain for him what he otherwise might not gain. The prayers of the church were to him as significant in the work of the kingdom, as the power of God.

Who can say what power a church could develop and exercise if it gave itself to the work of prayer, day and night, for the coming of the kingdom, for God's power on His servants and His word, for the glorifying of God in the salvation of souls? Most churches think their members are gathered into one simply to take care of and build up each other. They do not know that God rules the world by the prayers of His saints; that prayer is the power by which Satan is conquered; that by prayer the church on earth has authority over the powers of the heavenly world. They do not remember that Jesus has, by His promise, consecrated every assembly in His Name to be a gate of heaven, where His presence is to be felt and His power experienced as the Father fulfills their desires.

There will be great blessing when God's people meet as one in the Name of Jesus, to have His presence in the midst of a body all united in the Holy Spirit, and boldly claim the promise that it shall be done of the Father what they agree to ask.

"LORD, TEACH US TO PRAY."

Blessed Lord, who didst in Thy high-priestly prayer ask so earnestly for the unity of Thy people, teach us how Thou dost invite and urge us to this unity by Thy precious promise given to united prayer. It is when we are one in love and desire that our faith has Thy presence and the Father's answer.

O Father, we pray for Thy people, and for every smaller circle of those who meet together, that they may be one. Remove, we pray, all selfishness and self-interest, all narrowness of heart and estrangement by which that unity is hindered. Cast out the spirit of the world and the flesh, through which Thy promise loses all its power. Let the thought of Thy presence and the Father's favor draw us all nearer to each other.

Grant especially, blessed Lord, that Thy Church may believe that it is by the power of united prayer that she can bind and loose in heaven; that Satan can be cast out; that souls can be saved; that mountains can be removed; that the kingdom can be hastened. And grant, good Lord, that in the circle with which I pray, the prayer of the Church may indeed be the power through which Thy Name and Word are glorified. Amen.

CHAPTER FIVE

The Power of Persevering Prayer

> And he spake a parable unto them to the end that they ought always to pray, and not to faint. . . . And the Lord said, Hear what the unrighteous judge saith. And shall not God avenge his own elect, which cry to him day and night, and he is long-suffering over them? I say unto you, that he will avenge them speedily.—Luke 18:1-8

Of all the mysteries of prayer, the need for perseverance is one of the greatest. That the Lord, so loving and longing to bless, should have to be supplicated time after time, sometimes year after year, before the answer comes, we cannot easily understand. It is also one of the greatest practical difficulties in the exercise of believing prayer. When, after persevering supplication, our prayer remains unanswered, it is often easiest for our slothful flesh (and it has all the appearance of pious submission) to think that we must now cease praying because God may have a secret reason for withholding His answer to our request.

By faith alone the difficulty is overcome. When faith has taken its stand upon God's Word and the Name of Jesus, and has yielded itself to the leading of the Spirit to seek only God's will and honor in its prayer, it need not be discouraged by delay. It knows from Scripture that the power of believing prayer is simply irresistible; *real faith can never be disappointed.* It knows how, just as water, to exercise the irresistible power it can have; it must be gathered up and accumulated until the stream can come down in full force.

There must often be a heaping up of prayer until God sees that the measure is full, and the answer comes. Faith knows that, just as the plowman must take ten thousand steps and sow ten thousand seeds in preparation for the final harvest, so there is a need for oft-repeated persevering prayer in order to receive some desired blessing. Faith knows for certain that not a single believing prayer fails to have effect in heaven; each has influence, and is treasured up to work out an answer in due time to him who perseveres to the end.

Faith knows that it does not depend on human thoughts or possibilities, but on the Word of the living God. Even as Abraham through so many years "in hope believed against hope," and then "through faith *and patience* inherited the promise," faith believes that the long-suffering of the Lord is salvation, *waiting* and *hasting* unto the coming of its Lord to fulfill His promise.

Try to understand the two words in which our Lord sets forth the character and conduct, not of the unjust judge, but of our God and Father, toward those whom He allows to cry day and night to Him: "He is long-suffering over them; he will avenge them *speedily*." This will enable you, when the answer to your prayer does not come at once, to combine quiet patience and joyful confidence in your persevering prayer.

"He will avenge them *speedily*," the Master says. The blessing is all prepared; He is not only willing but eager to give them what they ask; everlasting love burns with the desire to reveal itself fully to His beloved, and to satisfy needs. God will not delay one moment longer than is absolutely necessary. He will do all in His power to hasten and speed the answer.

But, if this is true and His power is infinite, why must we often wait so long for the answer to prayer? And why must God's own elect so often, in the midst of suffering and conflict, cry day and night? "He is *long-suffering* over them."

"Behold! the husbandman waiteth for the precious fruit of the earth, being *long-suffering* over it, till it receive the early and the latter rain." The husbandman longs for his harvest, but knows that it must have its full season of sunshine and rain, so he waits patiently. A child so often wants to pick the half-ripe fruit; the husbandman waits till the proper time.

Man, in his spiritual nature too, is under the law of gradual growth that controls all created life. Only in the path of development can he reach his divine destiny. It is the Father, in whose hands are the times and seasons, who alone knows the moment when the soul or the Church is ripened to that fullness of faith in which it can take and keep the blessing. As a father who longs to have his only child home from school, and yet waits patiently till the time of training is completed, so it is with God and His children; He is the long-suffering One, and answers speedily.

Recognition of this truth leads the believer to cultivate the corresponding dispositions; *patience* and *faith, waiting* and *hasting*, are the secret of perseverance. By faith in the promise of God, we know that we *have* the petitions we have asked of Him. Faith takes and holds the answer in the promise as an unseen spiritual possession; faith rejoices in it and praises for it.

But there is a difference between the faith

that holds the word and knows it has the answer, and the clearer, fuller, riper faith that obtains the promise as a present experience. It is in persevering, confident, and praising prayer that the soul grows up into full union with its Lord in which it can experience possession of the blessing in Him. There may be in things around us, there may be in the great system of being of which we are part, there may be in God's government things that have to be put right through our prayer, so the answer can fully come.

The faith that has, according to the command, believed that it has received can allow God to take His time; it knows it has prevailed and must prevail. In quiet, persistent, and determined perseverance it continues in prayer and thanksgiving until the blessing comes. The combination appears so contradictory: the faith that rejoices in the answer of the unseen God as a present possession, and the patience that cries day and night until it is revealed. The *speedily* of God's *long-suffering* is witnessed by the triumphant but patient faith of His waiting child.

The great danger in this school of the answer delayed is the temptation to think that it may not be God's will to give us what we ask. If our prayer is according to God's Word, and under the leading of the Spirit, let us not give way to such fear. Learn to give God time. God needs time with us. If we only give Him time in our daily fellowship with himself for Him to exercise the full influence of His presence on us; and time, day by day, in the course of our waiting for faith to prove its reality and to fill our whole being, He himself will lead us from faith to vision; we shall see the glory of God.

Let no delay shake our faith. Of faith the saying holds true: "first the blade, then the ear, then the full corn in the ear." Each believing prayer is a step nearer the final victory. Each believing prayer helps to ripen the fruit and bring us nearer to it; it fills up the measure of prayer and faith known to God alone; it conquers the hindrances in the unseen world; it hastens the end.

Child of God, give the Father time. He is long-suffering over you. He wants the blessing to be rich, full, and sure. Give Him time while you cry day and night. Only remember the word, "I say unto you, he will avenge them speedily."

The blessing of persevering prayer is unspeakable. There is nothing so heart-searching as the prayer of faith. It teaches you to discover and confess and give up everything that hinders the coming of the blessing—everything may not be in accordance with the Father's will. It leads to closer fellowship with Him who alone can teach to pray; it leads to greater surrender to draw nigh under no covering but that of the blood and the Spirit. It calls to a closer and more simple abiding in Christ alone.

Christian, give God time. He will perfect that which concerns you. "Long-suffering—speedily" is God's watchword as you enter the gates of prayer; let it be yours too.

All labor, physical and mental, needs time and effort; we must give *ourselves* to it. Nature reveals her secrets and yields her treasures only to diligent and thoughtful labor. However little we can understand it, in spiritual husbandry it is the same: the seed we sow in the soil of heaven, the efforts we put forth, and the influence we seek to exert in the world above need our whole being. We must *give ourselves* to prayer. But let us hold fast the great confidence that in due season we shall reap if we faint not.

Let us learn the lesson as we pray for the Church of Christ. She is as the poor widow, in the absence of her Lord, apparently at the mercy of her adversary, helpless to retaliate. Let us, when we pray for His Church, or any portion of it, under the power of the world, asking Him to visit her with the mighty workings of His Spirit and to prepare her for His coming, let us pray with assured faith.

Prayer does help, praying always and not fainting will bring the answer. Only give God time. And then keep crying day and night. "Hear what the righteous judge saith. And shall not God avenge his own elect, which cry to him day and night, and *he is long-suffering* over them. I say unto you, *He will avenge them speedily.*"

"LORD, TEACH US TO PRAY."

O Lord my God, teach me now to know Thy way and in faith to understand what Thy Beloved Son has taught: "He will avenge them speedily." Let Thy tender love, and the delight Thou hast in hearing and blessing Thy children, lead me implicitly to accept Thy promise—that we receive what we believe, that we have the petitions we ask, and that the answer will in due time be seen.

Lord, I understand the seasons in nature, and know to wait with patience for the fruit I long for. Oh, fill me with the assurance that Thou wilt delay not one moment longer than is needed, and that faith will hasten the answer.

Blessed Master, Thou hast said that it is a sign of God's elect that they cry day and night. Oh, teach me to understand this. Thou knowest how speedily I grow faint and weary. It is as if the Divine Majesty is so much beyond the need or the reach of continued supplication that it does not become me to be too importunate. O Lord, do teach me how real the labor of prayer is. Here on earth when I have failed in an undertak-

ing, I can often succeed by renewed and more continuing effort, by giving more time and thought; show me how, by giving myself more entirely to prayer, to live in prayer, I shall obtain what I ask.

Above all, my blessed teacher, author and perfecter of faith, by Thy grace let my whole life be one of faith in the Son of God who loved me and gave himself for me—in whom my prayer gains acceptance, in whom I have the assurance of the answer, in whom the answer will be mine. Lord Jesus, in this faith I will pray always and not faint. Amen.

CHAPTER SIX

The All-Prevailing Plea

> Whatsoever ye shall ask *in my name*, that will I do. If ye shall ask me anything *in my name*, that will I do. That whatsoever ye shall ask the Father *in my name*, he may give it you. Verily, verily, I say unto you, If ye shall ask anything of the Father, he will give it you *in my name*. Hitherto ye have asked nothing *in my name*: ask, and ye shall receive. In that day ye shall ask *in my name*.—John 14:13, 14; 15:16; 16:23, 24, 26.

The disciples until this time had not asked in the Name of Christ, nor had He himself ever used the expression. The nearest approach is "met together in my name." Here in His parting words, Jesus repeats the word unceasingly in connection with promises of unlimited meaning—*"whatsoever," "anything," "what ye will"*

—to teach them and us that His Name is our only and all-sufficient plea. The power of prayer and the answer depend on the right use of the Name.

What is a person's name? It is the word or expression by which the person is represented to us. When I mention or hear a name, it calls up before me the whole man, what I know of him, and also the impression he has made on me. The name of a king includes his honor, his power, his kingdom. His name is the symbol of his power.

Each name of God embodies and represents some aspect of the glory of the Unseen One; and the Name of Christ is the expression of all He has done and all He is and lives to do as our Mediator.

And what is it to take action in the name of another? It is to come with the power and authority of that person, as his representative and substitute. Such a use of another's name always supposes a mutual trust; no one would give another the free use of his name without first being assured that his honor and interest were as safe with that person as with himself.

And what is it when Jesus gives us the free use of His Name, with the assurance that whatever we ask in it will be given to us? The ordinary comparison of one person giving another, on some special occasion, the liberty to ask something in his name becomes insufficient here, for Jesus solemnly gives to *all* His disciples general and unlimited use of His Name at *all* times for *all* they desire. He could not do this if He could not trust us with His interests, not knowing if His honor would be safe in our hands. The free use of the name of another is always the token of great confidence, of close union. He who gives his name to another stands aside to let that other act for him; he who takes the name of another gives up his own as of no value. When I go in the name of another, I deny myself, taking not only his name but himself and what he is instead of myself and what I am.

Such a use of a person's name may be in virtue of *a legal union*. A businessman leaving his home and business gives his manager a general power by which he can draw thousands of dollars in the employer's name. The manager does this not for himself but only in the interests of the business. It is because the owner knows and trusts him as wholly devoted to his interests and business that he dares put his name and property at his command.

When the Lord Jesus went to heaven, He left His work, the management of His kingdom on earth, in the hands of His servants. He gave them His Name to draw all the supplies they needed for the due conduct of His business. And they have the spiritual power to avail themselves of the Name of Jesus only to the extent to which they yield themselves to live only for the interests and the work of the Master. The use of the Name always supposes the surrender of our interests to Him whom we represent.

Such a use of the Name may also be in virtue of a *life union*. In the case of the businessman and his manager, the union is temporary. But we know how oneness of life on earth gives oneness of name—a child has the father's name because he has his life. Often the child of a good father has been honored or helped by others because of the name he bore. But this would not last long if it were discovered that it was only a name and that the father's character was wanting. The name and the character or spirit must be in harmony. When such is the case, the child will have a double claim on the father's friends; this character secures and increases the love and esteem initially received because of the name.

So it is with Jesus and the believer. We are one, we have one life, one Spirit with Him; for this reason we may come in His Name. Our power in using that Name, whether with God, or men, or devils, *depends on the measure of our spiritual life-union.* The use of the name rests on the unity of life; the Name and the Spirit of Jesus are one.*

The union that empowers one to use the Name may also be *the union of love.* When a bride whose life has been one of poverty becomes united to the bridegroom, she gives up her own name, to be called by his, and receives the full right to use it. She purchases in his name, and that name is not refused. This is done because the bridegroom has chosen her for himself, counting on her to care for his interests; the two are now one.

The Heavenly Bridegroom could do nothing less; having loved us and made us one with himself, what could He do but give those who bear His Name the right to present it before the Father, or to come with it to himself for all they need? There is no one who abandons himself to live in the Name of Jesus who does not receive, in ever-increasing measure, the spiritual capacity to ask and receive in that Name what he will. The bearing of the name of another supposes my having given up my own, and with it my own independent life; but then, I have taken, instead of my own, possession of all there is in the name.

Such illustrations show the defectiveness of the common view of a messenger sent to ask in the name of another, or a guilty one appealing to the name of a guarantor. Jesus himself is with the Father; it is not an absent one in whose name we pray. Even when we pray to Jesus himself, it must be in His Name. The name represents the person; to ask in the Name is to ask in full union of interest, life, and love with himself as one who lives in and for Him.

If the Name of Jesus has undivided supremacy in my heart and life, my faith will gain the assurance that what I ask in that Name cannot be refused. The name and the power of asking go together; when the Name of Jesus has become the power that rules my life, power in prayer with God will be seen too.

Everything depends on our own relation to the Name; the power it has on my life is the power it will have in my prayers. There is more than one expression in Scripture which can make this clear to us. When it says, *"Do all* in the name of the Lord Jesus," we see how this is the counterpart of the other, *"Ask all."* Doing all and asking all in His Name go together.

When we read, "We shall walk in the name of our God," we see that the power of the Name must rule in the whole life; only then will we have power in prayer. God looks not at the lips but at the life to see what the Name is to us. When Scripture speaks of "men who have given their lives for the name of the Lord Jesus," or of one "ready to die for the name of the Lord Jesus," we see what our relation to the Name must be; when it is everything to me, it will obtain everything for me. If I let it have all I have, it will let me have all it has.

"Whatsoever ye shall ask in my name, that will I do." Jesus means the promise literally. Christians have sought to limit it—it looks too free; it is hardly safe to trust man so unconditionally. However, the condition "in my name" is its own safeguard. It is a spiritual power which no one can use further than he obtains the capacity for, by his living and acting in that Name. As we bear that Name before men, we have power to use it before God.

We must plead for God's Holy Spirit to show us what the Name means, and what the right use of it is. It is through the Spirit that the Name, which is above every name in heaven, will take the place of supremacy in our heart and life too.

Disciples of Jesus, let the lessons of this day enter deep into your hearts. The Master says, "Only pray in my Name; whatever you ask will be given."

Heaven is open to you; the treasures and powers of the world of the spirit are placed at your disposal on behalf of men around you. Come and learn to pray in the Name of Jesus. As to the disciples, He says to us, "Hitherto ye have not asked in my name: ask, and ye shall receive."

Let each disciple of Jesus seek to avail himself of the rights of his royal priesthood and use the power placed at his disposal. Let Christians awake and hear the message: your prayer can obtain what otherwise will be withheld and can accomplish what otherwise remains undone. Awake and use the Name of Jesus to open the treasures of heaven for this perishing world.

Learn as the servants of the King to use His Name. "*Whatsoever* ye shall ask in my name, *that will I do.*"

"LORD, TEACH US TO PRAY."

Blessed Lord, it is as if each lesson Thou givest me has such fullness and depth of meaning, that if I can only learn this one, I shall know how to pray aright. This day I felt again as if I needed but one prayer every day: Lord! teach me what it is to pray in Thy Name. Teach me to live and act, to walk and speak, all in the Name of Jesus that my prayer cannot be anything else but in that blessed Name too.

And teach me, Lord, to hold fast the precious promise that whatsoever *we ask in Thy Name, Thou wilt do, the Father will give. I do not yet fully understand, and still less have fully attained, the wondrous union Thou meanest when Thou sayest "in my name," yet I would hold fast the promise until it fills my heart with the undoubting assurance—anything in the Name of Jesus.*

O my Lord, let Thy Holy Spirit teach me this. Thou didst say of Him, "The Comforter, whom the Father shall send in my name." He knows what it is to be from heaven in Thy Name, to reveal and to honor the power of that Name in Thy servants, to use that Name alone, and so to glorify Thee. Lord Jesus, let Thy Spirit dwell in me and fill me. I do yield my whole being to His rule and leading. Thy Name and Thy Spirit are one; through Him Thy Name will be the strength of my life and my prayer. Then I shall be able for Thy Name's sake to forsake all, in Thy Name to speak to men and to God, and to prove that this is indeed the Name above every name.

Lord Jesus, teach me by Thy Holy Spirit to pray in Thy Name. Amen.

---

*"Whatsoever ye shall ask in my name," that is, in my *nature*; for things of God are named according to their nature. We ask in Christ's Name, not when at the end of some request ("This I ask in the Name of Jesus Christ."), but when we pray *according to His nature*, which is love, which seeks not its own but only the will of God and the good of all creatures. Such asking is the cry of His own Spirit in our hearts (*The New Man* by Jukes).

CHAPTER SEVEN

The Holy Spirit and Prayer

> *In that day* ye shall ask me nothing. Verily, verily, I say unto you, *Whatsoever ye shall ask* the Father in my name, he will give it you. *Hitherto* have ye asked nothing in my name: ask, and *ye shall receive*, that your joy may be full. . . . *At that day* ye shall ask in my name: and I say not unto you, that I will pray the Father for you: for the Father himself loveth you.—John 16:23-26
>
> Praying in the Holy Spirit, keep yourselves in the love of God.—Jude 20, 21

The words of John (1 John 2:12-14) to little children, to young men, and to fathers, suggest that there are in the Christian life three main stages of experience: The first, that of the new-born child, with the assurance and the joy of forgiveness. The second, the transition stage of struggle and growth in knowledge and strength; young men growing strong, God's Word doing its work in them and giving them victory over the evil one. And then the final stage of maturity and ripeness: the fathers, who have entered deeply into the knowledge and fellowship of the Eternal One.

In Christ's teaching on prayer there also appear to be three stages in the prayer life, somewhat analogous. In the Sermon on the Mount we have the initial stage; in it, His teaching is all comprised in one word "Father." Pray to your Father, your Father sees, hears, knows, and will reward—*how much more* than any earthly father! Only be childlike and trustful.

Later on comes something like the transition stage of conflict and conquest, in words like these: "This sort goeth not out but by fasting and prayer"; "Shall not God avenge his own elect who cry day and night unto him?"

Finally we have in the parting words a higher level. The children have become men; they are now the Master's friends, from whom He keeps no secrets, to whom He says, "All things that I heard from my Father I made known unto you." To these, in the oft-repeated "whatsoever ye will," He hands over the keys of the kingdom. Now the time has come for the power of prayer in His Name to be proved.

The contrast between this final stage and the

previous preparatory ones is marked distinctly in the words we are to meditate on "Hitherto ye have asked nothing in my name"; "At that day ye shall ask in my name." We know what "at that day" means. It is the day of the outpouring of the Holy Spirit.

The great work Christ was to do on the cross, the mighty power and the complete victory to be manifested in His resurrection and ascension, were to result in the coming down from heaven, as never before, of the glory of God to dwell in men. The Spirit of the glorified Jesus was to come and be the life of His disciples. One of the marks of that wonderful Spirit-dispensation was to be a power in prayer previously unknown— prayer in the Name of Jesus, asking and obtaining whatsoever they would, a manifestation of the Spirit's indwelling.

To understand how the coming of the Holy Spirit was indeed to commence a new epoch in the prayer world, we must remember who He is, what His work is, and the significance of His not being given until Jesus was glorified. It is in the Spirit that God exists, for He is Spirit. It is in the Spirit that the Son was begotten of the Father; it is in the fellowship of the Spirit that the Father and the Son are one. It is through the Spirit that this communion of life and love is maintained—the eternal giving to the Son which is the Father's prerogative, and the eternal ask-

ing and receiving which is the Son's right and
blessedness. It has been so from all eternity. It is
especially so now, when the Son as Mediator
ever lives to pray.

The great work which Jesus began on earth of
reconciling in His own body God and man, He
carries on in heaven. To accomplish this, He
took up into His own person the conflict between
God's righteousness and our sin. On the cross He
once for all ended the struggle in His own body.
He then ascended to heaven that He might in
His body continually carry out the deliverance
and manifest the victory He had obtained. For
this purpose He ever lives to pray; in His unceasing intercession He places himself in living fellowship with the unceasing prayer of His redeemed ones. In fact, it is His unceasing intercession which shows itself in their prayers, and
gives them a power they never had before.

Christ does this through the Holy Spirit. The
Holy Spirit, the Spirit of the glorified Jesus, had
not come (John 7:39), and could not, until Jesus
had been glorified. This gift of the Father was
something distinctively new, entirely different
from what Old Testament saints had known.
Christ's entry within the veil, the redemption of
our human nature into fellowship with His
power and glory, and the union of our humanity
in Christ with the Three-One God were of such
inconceivable significance, that the Holy Spirit,

who had come from Christ's exalted humanity to testify in our hearts of what Christ had accomplished, was indeed no longer only what He had been in the Old Testament.

It was literally true the Holy Spirit was "not yet," for Christ was not yet glorified. He came now, first as the Spirit of the glorified Jesus. The Son, who was from eternity God, had entered upon a new existence as man, and returned to heaven with glory He did not have before. So also, the Blessed Spirit, whom the Son, on His ascension, received from the Father (Acts 2:33) into His glorified humanity, came to us with a new life, which He had not previously been able to give. Under the Old Testament He was invoked as the Spirit of God; at Pentecost He descended as the Spirit of the glorified Jesus, bringing down and communicating to us the full fruit and power of the accomplished redemption.

The continued efficacy and application of the redemption is maintained in the intercession of Christ. And it is through the Holy Spirit descending from Christ to us that we are drawn up into the great stream of His ever-ascending prayers. The Spirit prays for us without words. In the depths of our hearts where even thoughts are at times formless, the Spirit takes us up into the wonderful flow of the life of the Three-One God. Through the Spirit, Christ's prayers become ours, and ours are made His; we ask what we will, and it is given to us. We then understand from experience, "Hitherto ye have not asked in my name." "*At that day* ye shall ask in my name."

Brother, what you need to pray for in the Name of Christ, that your joy may be full is the baptism of this Holy Ghost. This is more than the Spirit of God under the Old Testament. This is more than the Spirit of conversion and regeneration the disciples had before Pentecost. This is more than the Spirit with a measure of His influence and working. This is the Holy Spirit, the Spirit of the glorified Jesus in His exaltation-power, coming on you as the Spirit of the indwelling Jesus, revealing the Son and the Father within (John 14:16-23).

When this Spirit is the Spirit not of our hours of prayer but of our whole life and walk, when He glorifies Jesus in us by revealing the completeness of His work, and by making us wholly one with Him and like Him, then we can pray in His Name, because we are indeed one with Him. Then we have that immediate access to the Father of which Jesus says, "I say not that I will pray the Father for you." We need to understand and believe that to be filled with the Spirit of the glorified One is the one need of God's believing people. Then shall we understand what it is, "with all prayer and supplication to be praying at all seasons in the Spirit," and what it is, "praying in the Holy Ghost, to keep ourselves in the love of God." "*At that day* ye shall ask in my name."

What our prayer avails depends upon what we are and what our life is. Living in the Name of Christ is the secret of praying in the Name of Christ; living in the Spirit fits us for praying in the Spirit. Abiding in Christ gives the right and power to ask what we will; the extent of the abiding is the exact measure of the power in prayer.

It is the Spirit dwelling within us that prays, not in words and thoughts always, but in a breathing and a being deeper than utterance. As much as there is of Christ's Spirit in us so is real prayer.

Let our lives be full of Christ and full of His Spirit, and the wonderfully unlimited promises to our prayer will no longer appear strange. "Hitherto ye have asked nothing in my name. Ask, and ye shall receive, that your joy may be full. At that day ye shall ask in my name. Verily, verily, I say unto you, Whatsoever ye shall ask the Father in my name, he will give it you."

"LORD, TEACH US TO PRAY."

O my God, in holy awe I bow before Thee, the Three in One. Again I have seen how the mystery of prayer is the mystery of the Holy Trinity. I adore the Father who ever hears and the Son who ever lives to pray. I adore the Holy Spirit who proceeds from the Father and the Son, to lift us up into the fellowship of that ever-blessed, never-ceasing asking and receiving. I bow, my God, in adoring worship, before the infinite condescension that, through the Holy Spirit, takes us and our prayers into the divine life and its fellowship of love.

My Blessed Lord Jesus, teach me to understand Thy lesson, that it is the indwelling Spirit, streaming from Thee, uniting to Thee, who is the Spirit of prayer. Teach me to become an empty, wholly consecrated vessel, to yield myself to His being. Teach me to honor and trust Him, as a living person, to lead my life and my prayer. Teach me especially in prayer to wait in holy silence and give Him place to breathe within me His unutterable intercession.

Teach me that through Him it is possible to pray without ceasing and to pray without failing, because He makes me partaker of the never-ceasing and never-failing intercession in which Thou, the Son, dost appear before the Father. Lord, fulfill in me Thy promise, "At that day ye shall ask in my name. Verily, verily, I say unto you, Whatsoever ye shall ask the Father in my name, that will he give." Amen.

CHAPTER EIGHT

Christ, the Intercessor

But I have prayed for thee, that thy faith fail not.—Luke 22:32

I say not unto you, that I will pray the Father for you.—John 16:26

He ever liveth to make intercession.—Heb. 7:25

All growth in the spiritual life is dependent upon clearer insight into what Jesus is to us. The more I realize that Christ must be all to me and in me, that all in Christ is indeed for me, the more I learn to live the real life of faith—dying to self, thus living wholly in Christ. The Christian life is no longer a vain struggle to live right, but is resting in Christ and finding strength in Him as my life, to fight the fight and gain the victory of faith. This is especially true of the life of prayer.

Prayer also comes under the law of faith, and when seen in the light of the fullness and completeness in Jesus, the believer understands that it no longer needs to be a matter of strain or anxious care; it is an experience of what Christ will do for him and in him—a participation in the life of Christ which, as on earth so in heaven, ever ascends to the Father as prayer. He can begin to pray, not only trusting in the merits of Jesus, or in the intercession by which our unworthy prayers are made acceptable, but in that union in which He prays in us and we in Him.*

The whole of salvation is Christ himself: He has given *himself* to us; He himself lives in us. Because He prays, we pray too. As the disciples, when they saw Jesus pray, asked Him to make them partakers of what He knew of prayer, so we, now that He is our intercessor on the throne, know that He makes us participate with himself in the life of prayer.

This is illustrated clearly in the last night of His life. In His high-priestly prayer (John 17), He shows us how and what He prays to the Father, and will pray when once ascended to heaven. Yet, in His parting address, He repeatedly associated His going to the Father with *their* new life of prayer. The two would be ultimately connected; His entrance on the work of His eternal intercession *would be the commencement and the power of their new prayer life in His Name.*

The sight of Jesus in His intercession gives us power to pray in His Name. All right and power of prayer is Christ; we share in His intercession.

To understand this, think first of *His intercession*—"He ever liveth to make intercession." The work of Christ on earth as Priest was but a beginning—as Aaron He shed His blood; as Melchizedek, He now lives within the veil to continue His work in the power of the eternal life.

As Melchizedek is more glorious than Aaron, so it is in intercession that the atonement has its true power and glory. "It is Christ that died: *yea more*, who is even at the right hand of God, who maketh intercession for us." That intercession is an intense reality, a work that is absolutely necessary and without which the continued application of redemption cannot take place.

In the incarnation and resurrection of Jesus, the wondrous reconciliation took place; man became partaker of the divine life and blessedness. But the personal appropriation of this reconciliation in each of His members here below cannot take place without the unceasing exercise of divine power by the head in heaven. In all conversion and sanctification, in every victory over sin and the world, there is a manifestation of the power of God.

This exercise of His power takes place only through His prayer. He asks of the Father, and receives from the Father. "*He is able* to save to the uttermost, *because* he ever liveth to make intercession." There is not a need of His people which He conveys in intercession that the Godhead can deny: His mediation on the throne is as real and indispensable as on the cross. Nothing takes place without His intercession. It engages all His time and powers; it is His unceasing occupation at the right hand of the Father.

We participate not only in the benefits of this His work but in the work itself, because we are His body. Body and members are one—"The head cannot say to the feet, I have no need of thee." We share with Jesus in all He is and has—"The glory which thou gavest me, I have given them." We are partakers of His life, His righteousness, His work. We share with Him in His intercession too; it is not a work He does without us.

We do this because we are partakers of His life—"Christ is our life"; "No longer I, but Christ liveth in me." The life in Him and in us is one and the same. His life in heaven is an *ever-praying* life. When it descends and takes possession of us, it does not lose its character; in us too it is the *ever-praying* life—a life that without ceasing asks and receives from God.

Do not mistakenly think there are two separate currents of prayer rising upwards, one from Him and one from His people. The substantial life-union is also prayer-union; what He prays passes through us, what we pray passes through Him. He is the angel with the golden censer. "*Unto him* there was given much incense," the secret of acceptable prayer, "that he should add it unto the prayers of all the saints upon the golden altar." We live and abide in Him, the Interceding One.

The Only-begotten is the only one who has the right to pray; to Him alone it was said, "Ask, and it shall be given thee." As in all other things the fullness dwells in Him, including true prayerfulness. He alone has the power of prayer.

Growth of the spiritual life consists in the clearer insight that all the treasures are *in Him*, and that we too are *in Him* to receive each moment what we possess in Him, grace for grace. So with the prayer life too. Faith in the intercession of Jesus must not only be that He prays in our stead, when we do not or cannot pray, but that, as the Author of our life and our faith, He enables us to pray in unison with himself. Our prayer must be a work of faith in this sense too. As we know that Jesus communicates His whole life in us, He also out of that prayerfulness, which is His alone, breathes into us our praying.

It is a new epoch in a believer's spiritual life when it is revealed to him how truly and entirely Christ is his life, standing as surety for His faithful and obedient. It is then that he begins to live a *faith-life*.

No less blessed will be the discovery that Christ is surety for our prayer life too, the center and embodiment of all prayer, which is communicated by Him through the Holy Spirit to His people. "He ever liveth to make intercession" as the head of the body, as the leader in that "new and living way" which He has opened up, as the "Author and the Perfecter" of our faith.

He provides in everything for the life of His redeemed ones by placing His own life in them; He cares for their life of prayer, by inducting up into His heavenly prayer life, by giving and maintaining His prayer life within them. "I have prayed for thee," not to render thy faith needless, but "that *thy faith* fail not"; our faith and prayer of faith is rooted in His.

"If ye abide in me," the everliving Intercessor, and pray with me and in me, "ask whatsoever ye will, and it shall be done unto you."

All these wonderful prayer promises have as their aim and their justification the glory of God in the manifestation of His kingdom and the salvation of sinners. As long as we chiefly pray for ourselves, the promises of His last night must remain a sealed book to us. It is to the fruit-bearing branches of the Vine; it is to disciples sent into the world as the Father sent Him, to live for perishing men; it is to His faithful servants and intimate friends who take up the work

He leaves behind, who have like their Lord become as the seedcorn, losing its life to multiply it manifold; it is to such that the promises are given.

We must each find out what our work is and whose souls are entrusted to our special prayers. Let us make our intercession for them our life of fellowship with God, and we shall not only find the promises of power in prayer made true to us, but we shall also begin to realize how our abiding in Christ and His abiding in us makes us share in His joy and blessing and saving men.

We not only owe everything to, but we are taken up as active partners and fellow-workers in this wonderful intercession of our Blessed Lord, Jesus. Now we understand what it is to pray in the Name of Jesus, and why it has such power—in His Name, in His Spirit, in himself, in perfect union with Him. When shall we be wholly taken up into this intercession of Christ, and always pray in it?

"LORD, TEACH US TO PRAY."

Blessed Lord, in lowly adoration I would again bow before Thee. Thy whole redemption work has now passed into prayer; all that now occupies Thee in maintaining and dispensing what Thou didst purchase with Thy blood is only prayer. Thou ever livest to pray. Because we are in Thee, the direct access to the Father is always open, our life can be one of unceasing prayer, and the answer to our prayer is sure.

Blessed Lord, Thou hast invited Thy people to be Thy fellow-workers in a life of prayer. Thou hast united thyself with Thy people and makest them as Thy body share with Thee in that ministry of intercession; through this alone the world can be filled with the fruit of Thy redemption and the glory of the Father. With more liberty than ever I come to Thee, my Lord, and beseech Thee, teach me to pray. Thy life is prayer, Thy life is mine. Lord, teach me to pray, in Thee, like Thee.

And my Lord, give me especially to know, as Thou didst promise Thy disciples, that Thou art in the Father, and I in Thee, and Thou in me. Let the uniting power of the Holy Spirit make my whole life an abiding in Thee and Thy intercession; let my prayer be its echo, that the Father may hear me in Thee and Thee in me. Lord Jesus, let Thy mind, in everything, be in me, and my life, in everything, be in Thee. So shall I be prepared to be the channel through which Thy intercession pours its blessing on the world. Amen.

Note

The new epoch of prayer in the Name of Jesus is pointed out by Christ as the time of the outpouring of the Spirit, in which the disciples enter upon a more enlightened apprehension of the economy of redemption, and become as clearly conscious of their oneness with Jesus as of His oneness with the Father. Their prayer in the Name of Jesus is now directly to the Father himself: "*I say not that I will pray* for you, for the Father himself loveth you," Jesus says. He had previously spoken of the Spirit's coming, "*I will pray* the Father, and he will give you the Comforter."

This prayer thus has as its central desire, our insight into our union with God in Christ (John 17:23: "I in them and thou in me"), so that in Jesus we behold the Father as united to us, and ourselves as united to the Father. Jesus Christ must be revealed to us, not only through the truth in the mind, but in our inmost personal consciousness, as the living personal reconciliation, as He in whom God's Fatherhood and Father-love have been perfectly united with human nature and it with God. Not that with the direct prayer to the Father, the mediatorship of Christ is set aside; but it is no longer viewed as something external, existing outside of us, but as a living spiritual existence within us, so that the Christ *for us*, the Mediator, has really become Christ *in us*.

—Beck of Tubingen

---

*On the difference between having Christ as an Advocate or Intercessor who stands outside of us, and having Him within us, see the note from Beck of Tubingen, above.

Books by Andrew Murray

ANDREW MURRAY CHRISTIAN MATURITY LIBRARY

The Believer's Absolute Surrender
The Believer's Call to Commitment
The Believer's Full Blessing of Pentecost
The Believer's New Covenant
The Believer's New Life
The Believer's Secret of a Perfect Heart
The Believer's Secret of Holiness
The Believer's Secret of Living Like Christ
The Believer's Secret of Obedience
The Believer's Secret of Spiritual Power
The Believer's Secret of the Master's Indwelling
The Spirit of Christ

ANDREW MURRAY PRAYER LIBRARY

The Believer's Prayer Life
The Believer's School of Prayer
The Ministry of Intercessory Prayer
The Secret of Believing Prayer

ANDREW MURRAY DEVOTIONAL LIBRARY

The Believer's Daily Renewal
The Believer's Secret of Intercession
The Believer's Secret of the Abiding Presence
The Believer's Secret of Waiting on God
Day by Day with Andrew Murray

How to Raise Your Children for Christ